Martin Luther King

WHO WAS...

Martin Luther King

The man who had a dream

LIZ GOGERLY

✱ SHORT BOOKS

First published in 2006 by
Short Books
3A Exmouth Office
London EC1R OJH

10 9 8 7 6 5 4 3 2 1

Copyright ©Liz Gogerly 2006

Liz Gogerly has asserted her right under the Copyright,
Designs and Patents Act 1988 to be identified as the author of this work.
All rights reserved. No part of this publication may be
reproduced, stored in a retrieval system or transmitted in any form,
or by any means (electronic, mechanical, or otherwise) without
the prior written permission of both the copyright owner
and the publisher.

A CIP catalogue record for this book
is available from the British Library.

Quiz by Sebastian Blake
ISBN 1-904977-65-0
(978-1-904977-65-0)

Printed in Great Britain by
Bookmarque Ltd, Croydon, Surrey

For Ash, with love

Chapter One

"It just isn't fair Daddy," croaked Yolanda. Her face was crumpled in disappointment, her eyes brimming with tears of frustration. "I want to go to Funtown. It has a roller coaster and lots of good rides. Why can't we go?"

"Come on Yoki-poky," Martin lifted his little girl on to his lap. He had to find a gentle way of explaining to Yoki why she couldn't go to Funtown. It wasn't because he didn't want to take her there – if only that were it! No, it was time to explain the situation to her properly.

"Funtown doesn't look so much fun to me,"

Martin reasoned. "How can it be fun if it doesn't allow all children to go there?"

"But Daddy, the ad on the TV said *everyone* was invited. And I want to go."

Martin kissed the top of Yoki's head. She was six years old now and had the whole world at her feet. Well, should have, he thought painfully. The truth was his children weren't free. They couldn't go to the same parks, picture houses or food counters as white children. Everywhere they went they were treated as second-class citizens. Yoki was only a shrimp but it was time to tell her the truth.

"It isn't easy to understand Yoki," Martin continued, "but in America there are laws that say where and how we should be. Many of those laws are unfair. They mean that Negro families can't go to some of the places that white people go."

"Why Daddy?" Yoki squirmed in his lap.

Martin admired his daughter's need for understanding. "It doesn't make much sense," he replied slowly. "These rules were made by the government. They say that Negroes and white people have to obey certain segregation laws which means that they have to use separate places or even things – take the water fountains for example."

"That's just silly, Daddy. What other things can't we use?" Yoki was puzzled.

"Well," Martin went on, "When you and I go on the bus then we have to sit on the seats at the back while white people sit at the front. Sometimes we even have to give up our seats for white people if there are not enough seats left."

"That isn't fair Daddy," wailed Yoki. "Why do we have to give up our seats to the white people? What if there was a really old person with a stick sitting at the back. Would they have to give up their seat to a white person too? That doesn't seem right to me."

Martin was taken aback by his little girl's gift for straight talking.

"It's the law, Yoki," Martin explained. "But just because it's the law now doesn't mean it'll always be the law. In my heart, I know one day that all children will be able to go where they like. Daddy knows this because he's fighting for it, honey."

Yoki was silent for a moment. Then, her eyes flashed with anger.

"But Daddy," her nostrils flared, "I want to go to Funtown *now*. I hate white people for not letting us go there."

Martin hugged her close. "I know, but we have to be patient, darling. And, we mustn't get angry. We have to find it in our hearts to be strong. God will help you to be strong. He'll help you to love the white man and believe that one day we'll join hands together to make a better world."

"Can we go to Funtown then?" Yoki's eyes brightened.

"Some time, we'll go to Funtown and all the other places you like the look of."

"If you say it can happen, Daddy, then I know it can," Yoki gave her father a little smile. She adored him. When he explained things to her she always felt better. And when he wrapped her in his big warm arms she knew that the world wasn't such a bad place. Yeah, she would love to ride the roller coaster today, but Daddy had promised that they could go another day.

It was with a heavy heart that Martin left the house that night for one of his meetings. As he took his car across town he watched the street scenes with more interest than usual. He passed a group of young people gathered at one street corner. They were sharing a joke and laughing. Tonight they looked carefree and happy. But, Martin thought sadly, tomorrow morning they would face the reality of another day. They would be up at dawn, then they'd probably walk a few miles to their place of employment. Many young men took jobs in hotels and restaurants as waiters or porters. All too often they sweated it out in factories or laboured on building sites. Otherwise, they did dirty work – like sweeping the streets or cleaning the public lavatories. It wasn't much better for the girls – they were often employed by white people to tidy their homes and look after their children. Martin felt saddened that such bright young people didn't have the opportunity to become professional working people. In a country they called the land of the free, they deserved better.

***

As Martin pulled up at the next halt sign, he

motioned an old man to cross the road. The man's blank expression gave way to a huge, friendly smile. Martin grinned back but couldn't help but notice how the poor man was so rickety on his legs that he struggled to walk. He was, thought Martin, just one of those many ageless characters that he saw everyday across town. He could be 40 or 70. It was impossible to say. A lifetime of hard work had taken away his youth and then his health. And for what? It hadn't made him rich. It hadn't brought him the security or the health care he needed in his old age either. In the richest nation in the world, he deserved more.

And, so it was that Martin's thoughts turned back to his daughter. Crushing Yoki's dream of going to Funtown pained him more that she would ever know. Watching the excitement drain from her little face was more agonizing than a punch in the stomach. The hurt he felt inside was for Yoki but it was also for the millions of other Negro children growing up in America. What kind of future did they have? As long as there was segregation and discrimination in jobs then they would always be second best. Martin was fighting for the freedom of all these children because they deserved a brighter future.

Chapter Two

Martin Luther King is perhaps the most famous dreamer in the world. On 28 August, 1963 he took the stage in front of more than 250,000 people who had gathered in the centre of Washington D.C. It was the largest crowd ever to attend a Civil Rights demonstration. On that hot summer day he told them about his dream of a free country for all people. His beautiful, honey-toned voice filled the muggy air that hung over the Lincoln Memorial. The words seemed to pour from him as he gave the world glimpses of his hopes and dreams of a free America. Part of his almighty vision was a land where his own children wouldn't have to face racism and prejudice: "I have a dream that my four little children will one day live in a nation where they will not be judged by the color [sic] of their skin but by the content of their character…"

People who heard Martin speak that day were moved to tears. They felt inspired, empowered and proud. The good doctor had spoken for them. He had conveyed all their dreams. He had become their voice. At long last they had a voice!

When Martin Luther King told the world about his dream for his own children he was partly speaking for the boy he had once been. He was born on 15 January, 1929 (he was christened Michael Luther King but changed his name to Martin). It was a time of confusion and deprivation for people from many walks of life in America. The Great Depression had begun, bringing unemployment, hunger and destitution to millions of people throughout the land. Martin Luther King was one of the lucky ones. His father, Martin Luther King Sr. was a pastor at Ebenezer Baptist Church in Atlanta. A bull-headed but loving man, he always made sure there was enough money for food on the table and warm clothes on his children's backs. Martin's mother, Alberta was a thoughtful and loving woman. She was always there with a warm hug and wise words. The family lived in a comfortable clapperboard house on Auburn Avenue. It was in the black area of Atlanta but it was a good, solid middle-class district.

Happy and healthy, Martin's childhood seemed blessed compared to many other young black lives. But, growing up in Atlanta, Georgia, in the American South, Martin could never be sheltered from the evil, deep-rooted claw that is racism.

"Why can't we be friends, Mummy?" Martin was six years old and fighting back the tears. That day his best buddy, his friend since he was three, had told him that they were no longer allowed to play together.

"His father has told him that now we've started different schools, we can't be friends," Martin fiddled idly with the knife and fork in front of him. He was looking down because he knew if he looked up then he would cry for real.

Alberta gave her husband a knowing look across

the table. This was the moment they had dreaded. The time was right to explain to little Michael just what kind of country he'd been born in. He needed to hear about segregation and the laws that kept people apart because of the colour of their skin. His friend was white. Little Martin was black. They were destined to live separate lives. Now Martin needed to know these things so he could be strong enough to cope with them.

"We don't like these laws," Daddy King went on, "but we have to live by them."

"In no way must you ever feel inferior, Michael," Alberta told him. "Never ever think that you're a nobody." Her face burned brightly as she took her son's face in her hands and looked intently into his eyes. "Michael, you are somebody special. Don't ever think that you're not as good as anyone else."

His mother's words hung in the air. If it is possible to physically reach up and gather words and clutch them close to your heart, then that is what young Martin did that day. Those words stayed with him all his life. He never felt inferior. Not even when he was eight years old and he was slapped by an angry white woman in a downtown store.

"I'm so angry," muttered Alberta as she hugged Martin close, "How dare that woman treat you like that."

"I didn't do anything, Mother. I didn't tread on her. She just shouted at me. 'Nigger', she called me. 'You stepped on my foot,' she said. I just…" Martin struggled to explain. "I just said nothing. I stared and then she slapped me."

"We're leaving now,' Alberta grabbed Martin's hand and whisked him out into the street. "Remember what I said?" she asked.

"I know, Mother," Martin replied. "I'm a somebody."

"Good boy." Alberta beamed.

"And not even that woman could make me feel like a nobody!"

***

"Nobody speaks to me like that," bellowed Daddy King.

It was a few years later and Martin watched as the

assistant at a shoe store tried to deal with his irate father. What had promised to be an ordinary trip to buy a pair of shoes had turned into a horrible hullabaloo, with all the puff and bluster coming from just one side – his father.

"These seats are empty," Martin Senior insisted. "I'm not sitting at the back when there's nothing wrong with the seats we're sitting in."

"I'm happy to serve you but you'll have to move to those seats in the rear of the shop," the assistant carried on politely.

"Then we'll take our custom elsewhere," Martin Senior replied, with all the authority he could muster. "I just can't stand being sent to the back," he complained later as they traveled home on the bus.

"I know daddy" said Martin, who couldn't help but notice that they were sitting at the back of the bus.

"I don't care how long I have to live with this system," Martin Senior hissed under his breath, "I will never accept it."

Young Martin was proud of his father. He liked the way he didn't stand back and accept the law. When he grew up he wanted to be like his Daddy. He wasn't going to allow people to tell him what to do either.

***

Martin did well at school. By nature he was curious and bombarded his parents and his teachers with questions, questions and more questions: "Why is there poverty?" he quizzed his stumped teachers. "How can we help the poor?" he asked his parents. "What am I going to do with my life? Can I help the poor?" he asked himself as he lay in bed at night.

Early on he realized the power of words. They held or swayed people. They could move you to tears, make you laugh until your guts hurt, rouse a storm of anger or calm the loudest rage. Words, quite simply, could change the world.

"One day," Martin thought, "I'm going to get me some big words."

"You did well, Martin," beamed Mrs Bradley, "Your father will be proud. You certainly have the gift for speaking in public."

Martin smiled back at his teacher. They were traveling back to Atlanta from a speaking contest in

Dublin, Georgia. That day Martin had scooped first prize. At fourteen years old, Martin was showing great promise in his studies. Carry on like he was and he'd be at Crozer Theological Seminary, the college for training priests and rabbis, before he knew it. Martin felt proud of his achievement but he didn't allow success to go to his head.

"Since I was little I've always wanted to speak well," Martin told Mrs Bradley.

"Well, you certainly did that today. I think you've got a future in public speaking, Martin."

As they talked, the bus they were travelling on came to a halt. A few people got on and shuffled down the aisle to take their places – the black people to the rear and the white people to the front. It was the way of life but Martin always hated the injustice of the system; and though it went unsaid, so did most black people.

"I'm glad the bus isn't full," said Mrs Bradley. "My poor old feet are on fire."

"My poor young feet are feeling the heat too," laughed Martin. It was the last laugh of the 90-mile journey. At the next stop, a pack of people mounted the bus. Suddenly, there weren't enough seats for the white passengers. That meant that the black passengers would have to give up their seats.

"Hey, get up off those seats," shouted the driver pointing to Martin and his teacher. "You know the law."

Martin and Mrs Bradley looked at each other. Mrs Bradley started to get up but Martin felt anger exploding through his veins. No way was he going to move. No way!

"Get up nigger boy!" the driver barked nastily.

Snap! Anger turned to fury. Martin fought hard to control himself. Nigger! It's just a word he told himself. Just a word… Just a word… The mantra seemed to quell his temper. Just a word, but boy, did words have the power to ignite rage. How dare that man speak to him like that, he thought. As Martin got up to let the white passenger take his seat, he felt the anger eat through every tissue of his being. His parents had taught him to rise above anger and hatred. They told him to love the white man. But, how did you love the white man when he treated you like scum?

Chapter Three

Where did a person find the love and wisdom to tackle racism? Religion certainly played its part. As the son and grandson of a preacher, Martin was brought up as a practising Christian. Daddy King wanted his eldest son to preach, too. As a teenager Martin wasn't sure if this was his destiny. Perhaps if he was a lawyer or a doctor he had more chance of doing good in the world. Nevertheless his Christian faith was important to him.

Ebenezer Baptist Church was on the corner of Jackson Street and Auburn Avenue in Atlanta. This was where Daddy King was pastor and to Martin it was a second home. The red-brick building could hold 800 people. Each Sunday a jolly crowd of worshippers wearing their best clothes tripped down the wine-coloured carpet to take their place in the pews. Daddy King thrilled them with his sermons.

"You will *all* find peace in the promised land," he'd proclaim in his large booming voice. The congregation whooped and cheered, filling the room with their hallelujahs and thanks. Later, the gospel choir would sing hearty Baptist hymns that filled people with joy. Singing, clapping, laughing – that was just as much part of the Sunday service as praying and listening to the pastor's wise words. Throughout America, similar scenes in all kinds of churches were taking place. Religion brought black people everywhere great comfort. Their faith gave them strength to put up with their lives.

The summer of 1944 was a testing time for young Martin. He was fifteen and spent his first time away from home. His parents had always encouraged him to take summer employment and this year he was off to Simsbury in Connecticut to work in the tobacco fields.

"Sure is hot today, Martin," said one of the other boys working the fields. "I can feel my back going already."

"Sure," answered Martin, wiping his brow, "but I'm enjoying myself too."

It was true. Martin was amazed by how different things were up here in Connecticut. For the first time in his life he'd tasted freedom and it was exhilarating. White folk seemed to treat Negroes with more respect here. Why, they could even eat in some of the fancy restaurants in Hartford.

"We actually used the main door at the theatre," Martin trilled. "A bunch of white and Negro kids all together. I just couldn't believe it. Then, we were allowed to sit anywhere we liked in the theatre. Can you imagine that happening back home?"

"Uh, huh," said the other lad shaking his head, "probably get a whippin'."

The boys chuckled but they both knew it was no laughing matter.

***

And, it was no laughing matter on the long train journey home from Connecticut either. As the locomotive chugged through New York and New Jersey, Martin took a place in the dining-car with all the other passengers. He sat watching the scenery go by, and couldn't help but feel that this is how life ought to be. Nobody was sent to the back.

But when the train reached the South, Martin felt a poke on his shoulder.

"Hey you, you sit over there." The waiter was firm and unfriendly.

"What?" Martin was genuinely puzzled.

"You're back in Dixie now, son. You know your place."

With that Martin was escorted to a table at the back. A curtain was swished shut, apparently so none of the white customers had to see a Negro eat his dinner! Martin sat behind the curtain. He was quietly fuming.

"Welcome back," he thought as he swallowed hard.

Chapter Four

"It's a fine family tradition," Daddy King almost sang out each word as he patted Martin on the shoulder.

"Your mother's father and I went to Morehouse College. And now you've passed the entrance examinations at just fifteen. I have high hopes for you, Martin. Maybe one day you'll follow me into the pulpit."

Martin still wasn't set on becoming a preacher and Morehouse seemed to open up a whole world of intellectual possibilities. First of all, however, Martin had some serious catching up to do. He might have passed the examinations to enroll at Morehouse but in actual fact his reading skills were below average.

"Why, I don't believe it," Alberta looked flabbergasted. "You can read better than an eighth grade kid."

"That's not what they reckon at college, Mother." Martin was flattened but not disheartened. "I'm not going to let that get in my way though."

"That's my boy," Alberta smiled, but Martin had other things on his mind.

"You know, it's just not right, Mother," he went on. "I'm intelligent. My teachers were good too. They just had too many children in their classes. They didn't have the right equipment or enough books. There's something wrong with a country that gives the best of everything to one group of people over another."

***

At Morehouse, Martin joined the football club, dated pretty girls and enjoyed the privileges of a college education. He never gave up questioning the racial situation in America. He read up on social politics, listened to the college lecturers, and yet he didn't find the answers he was looking for. Soon, Martin began doubting his religion. Reading up on the great philosophers and historians had made him question the truth of the Bible.

"I feel uncomfortable with the black church," he told his tutor. "All that stamping of feet and shouting. What does it achieve? It doesn't put food on the poor man's table, nor does it make the black community strong enough to fight for their rights."

Martin found some of the answers when he listened to his college professors.

"Behind the myths and legends of the Bible are many profound truths that we cannot escape," explained Professor Kelsey.

"Education liberates us all," said Doctor Mays. "We can change the system if we're educated."

Both men inspired and motivated Martin to do well. He walked away from Morehouse College with a bachelor of arts degree in sociology on 8 June, 1948. By this time he'd had a change of mind. Yes, he would be a minister like his father. He could make his sermons intellectually stimulating. And, who knows, perhaps he could use his position to change society, too.

***

After Morehouse came the prestigious Crozer Theological Seminary in Pennsylvania. This time Martin was set on a B.A in divinity.

"I'm looking forward to getting out of the South," Martin told his father. "And, Crozer is integrated. Just imagine that…"

Daddy King could imagine. He feared that his son would be badly treated. White people had ideas about Negroes. He didn't like to think about anybody calling his son a lazy nobody.

Martin wasn't about to be called a good-for-nothing by anyone, though – he made sure of that. Martin Luther King was a short man. What he lacked in height, however, he made up for in style. His shoes shone and his shirts were pristine. He also made sure that he behaved impeccably. He was up at the crack of dawn; he worked long and hard over his books; and he was never late for lectures. His hard work paid off. Martin became a grade A student. And he was learning more about religion, philosophy, politics and social politics, too.

"This man was all about love." Martin's face lit up as he spoke about the Indian leader, Mahatma Gandhi. Since he'd attended that lecture about Gandhi his thoughts had been on fire.

"Love is the answer!" Martin tried to explain to anyone who would listen. "When Gandhi wanted to protest against British rule he led a peaceful protest. He urged the people to use passive resistance. By loving the enemy instead of hating them, he brought about change. That's just what we could do here in America…"

***

"Hey, darkie, did you mess up my room?"

Shocked, Martin's eyes zapped up from the book he was reading. A terrifying whirlwind of male aggression had just stormed into his bedroom.

"Yeah you," puffed the student. "You think you're

so smart. I know you raided my room."

Martin got up slowly from his chair. "I don't know what you're talking about."

"Don't lie to me, nigger." The student's face was pink and venomous.

"Get out of my room," said Martin in a clipped tone. Loving the enemy wasn't always easy but Martin wasn't about to be rattled.

"So you think you're brave, do you?" the student went on. "Do you?" There was a mad glint in his eyes as he pulled out a pistol and waved it near Martin's head. "I'll shoot you King, make no bones."

"I told you I didn't do it." Martin remained calm.

"Hey put that gun down," said another student.

Suddenly there was a whole room of people urging the gunslinger to back off. When the crowd finally led the angry student away, Martin collapsed on his bed.

"You've got to press charges," insisted one of the students.

But Martin never did take up the case. Miraculously the gun-toting idiot calmed down. He even apologized to Martin and much later they became friends. Martin went on to become one of the most popular students on campus.

"There's something so warm about him," said one of the female students.

"You just fancy him," giggled her friend.

"No," the girl argued. "He's brave. He's clever and wise. I'd trust him with my life."

Chapter Five

Martin graduated from Crozer in the summer of 1951 with a B.A in divinity. He came top of his year and won a scholarship to Boston University to study for a doctorate in theology. By now the questions that had bothered him as a teenager had stepped up a gear. These days he wanted understanding about God and man. For this he needed more knowledge.

By nature he was a neat man but his room was always littered with books. The works of Hegel shared shelf space with Plato and Marx. Martin stayed up late, reading and borrowing ideas from these great men. From all his reading, one thing was certain in his mind: "War is senseless," he told his father. "I reject any kind of war. Surely, man must find another path. And that must be love and non-violence."

Still, Martin always found time to have fun. He moved into digs with his best friend Philip Lenund. They regularly put on their gladdest rags and went out to jazz clubs and other night spots. Neither of them had any problem attracting lovely girls. Martin and Philip also organized a Philosophy Club to meet at their place each weekend. As the coffee flowed and the teaspoons rattled, the debates stirred up new ideas in Martin's mind.

"I'm having the time of my life," Martin told his friend Mary Powell over lunch one day. "But, something is missing. I'd like to meet a nice girl – you know somebody who could share my life and my work."

"Well, I never thought I'd hear you say that!" Mary's hand slapped the table, her face a picture of disbelief.

"I'm serious, Mary," said Martin. "Do you know any nice, attractive young women?"

***

Mary knew a girl called Coretta Scott. When Martin met her he was sure she was the woman for him. They had their first date on a cold, wet February day in 1952. Martin picked her up in his green Chevy.

"It usually takes ten minutes to drive here from university," he told her. "Today I did it in seven minutes flat." Coretta laughed. He was certainly charming!

Martin took Coretta to a cafeteria for lunch. Throughout the meal Martin could hardly take his eyes off her. Coretta was quiet and shy by nature and felt quite anxious.

"So Coretta, that's enough about me," Martin pushed away his plate. For most of the meal he had told her all about his studies at University. He'd even talked about pacifism and capitalism. Some girls might have glazed over but Coretta's intelligent eyes had been alert.

"Well," Coretta felt her shoulders relax. She liked talking to Martin. "I was born and raised on a farm in Alabama. Now I'm studying music at the New England Conservatory. One day I'd like to be a singer."

Martin continued to stare at her. She was perfect.

The green Chevy chugged back up the hill to the conservatory. Coretta was sitting bolt upright in the passenger seat. Now that it was just the two of them in the car alone together, she was feeling tense and excited all at the same time. Martin was a lovely man. She liked listening to his rich, deep voice. Though he was religious he didn't preach. She liked that because she wasn't very religious herself.

"You know, Coretta," Martin's voice broke the silence. "You have everything I have ever wanted in a wife." Coretta blinked.

"The four things I would look for in a wife are character, intelligence, personality and beauty. And, you have all of them."

Coretta's bottom lip dropped in astonishment.

"But you can't say those things. Why, you don't really know me."

"When can I see you again, Coretta?" Martin ploughed on. "How about this weekend?"

"Do you know, I'm not sure." This had come as quite a shock to Coretta. "Do you mind if I check my diary?" she stuttered as she stepped out of his car. "Call me later."

Martin took Coretta to a party that Saturday night. Coretta noticed how other girls watched Martin. She felt herself falling for him, too. Later that night she slipped into his arms and prepared herself to fall in love. Little over a year later, they were married. They were both still studying, so Coretta couldn't be the full-time wife that Martin wanted. For a while they shared the household chores. But while they enjoyed their new life setting up home together in Boston, the future was very much on Martin's mind.

"You know, Coretta, living here in the north would be the easy option."

"How do you mean, darling?"

Coretta had promised Martin that she would give up her singing career when they married. She had also decided she would go wherever his work took them.

"I could take a job teaching at the university and we would be well looked after."

"But Martin deep in your soul I know you want to be a preacher."

It was true, Martin had been giving guest sermons at local churches and had built up a reputation as a speaker. He'd also been offered an interview to become the pastor of a church in Montgomery, Alabama. This would mean tearing themselves away from the comfortable life they shared in Boston.

"I feel so torn," said Martin. "I feel perhaps that I'm needed more in the South. The people have nothing and nobody to stand up for the injustices against them."

"I'll be right beside you, whatever you choose, Martin," Coretta reassured him as she stroked his arm gently.

***

Martin wowed the congregation at Dexter Avenue Baptist Church in Montgomery. Shortly afterwards he was offered the post.

"You do know what it means if we move back south, don't you Coretta?" Martin looked serious.

"The back of the bus, last in line for everything, you mean," Coretta gave him a grave, knowing look.

"Yes, and it means that's how it'll be for our children... when we have them,' he added.

"I can make myself happy there, don't worry," she soothed.

Daddy King was less than happy.

"Why, son?" he was angry and puzzled. "It's worse in Montgomery than it is here in Atlanta. The white folk are tough and mean there, boy."

"But Daddy, I think I can make a difference..." Martin had already accepted the position and wouldn't be swayed by his father.

Chapter Six

Martin and Coretta moved to Montgomery in September 1954. It had been a wrench leaving Boston but the young couple always counted their blessings. One of those blessings was Martin becoming pastor at such a fine place as Dexter Baptist Church. It was situated in downtown Montgomery. Some might say the little red-brick building with its bell tower looked insignificant compared to the fine white government buildings in the same street. "Not so," thought Martin. "It stands proud amongst the grandeur."

Coretta had made the most of their new home,

too. The white frame house had seven rooms and a porch at the front.

"I'm so pleased that the baby grand piano fits in," beamed Coretta.

"Oh Corrie," said Martin, giving her a hug, "I'm so pleased that you will still have music in your life. You deserve that much as you've given up so much. And, thank you for making our home such a warm and inviting place."

"We're a team Martin," said Coretta.

The early days at Montgomery were hard work for Martin. He was up at 5.30am each day so he could spend three hours writing his thesis before setting off to Dexter to begin church work. After work he returned home and completed another three hours on his thesis. In spring 1955, he was finally awarded the doctorate in theology. From now onwards he was known as Doctor Martin Luther King.

"That Doctor King is so charming." Ellie, one of the old ladies who visited Dexter Church, was talking with her friend, Penelope. "I just can't believe such a young man can be so confident and wise."

"I know, Ellie," agreed Penelope, nodding her head

enthusiastically. "He's turning this church around. People are coming from far and wide to hear him speak."

"My cousin's children were having problems with their marriage – spittin' and cursin' at each other – could hardly be in the same room together for five seconds," went on Ellie. "The good doctor spoke with them. Told them they must look for the true meaning of love. Look into themselves. Don't know how he did it but that young couple are still together with a little one on the way."

"What a fine man," said Penelope shaking her head. "He helps the old people, too. When Alfred Jackson had a problem getting paid, Doctor King spoke to Alfred's boss. The boss was a white man but the doctor wasn't afraid. Don't know how he did it but sure enough Alfred got his money!"

"And, now I hear he's setting up a social-action program at the church," went on Ellie. "He's trying to get committees together for this, that and the other."

"Oh, you mean that committee for helping the sick?" asked Penelope.

"Huh, huh," Ellie agreed. "And he's trying to get

sponsorship for some of the brighter children for high school. Anyway, I could just go on all day about that wonderful man but I've got beds to make and chicken to fry."

"Me too," said Penelope with a whoop. "But, one thing's for certain sure, that man has really made a difference round here."

Martin's conviction that he could make a difference to the lives of black people living in the South had been strengthened by events taking place all around him. In May 1954, the US Supreme Court had ruled that segregation was illegal in publicly funded schools. This ruling had been by no means easy. It had taken years of effort by the National Association for the Advancement of Colored [sic] People (NAACP). The group had been founded in 1910, and worked through the legal system to take cases about segregation and race to court. In this particular case, the NAACP had pleaded the case of a black pupil called Linda Brown of Topeka, Kansas, who had been barred from an all-white school. The Supreme Court's decision had sent out shock waves throughout America. This ruling would set in motion more cases against segregation. Martin believed that it was the beginning of the end for this terrible system.

In the South the backlash was felt almost instantly. Some white people were full of hatred and spite for Negroes – they would never accept integration. They called the day of the ruling "black Monday" and began fighting back.

The Ku Klux Klan, or KKK, was a secret organization formed by white southerners that used violence against blacks, Jews and other minority groups. Dressed in white robes and pointed hoods, the KKK beat up and lynched innocent people. As a boy, Martin had seen the handy work of the KKK for himself. Seeing an innocent man hanging dead from a tree was not something you could ever forget. Now the members of the KKK was stepping up their attacks again. Like any black person in the South Martin was scared but he was also getting fed up. It was time for change.

"We can't turn a blind eye to what is going on," urged Martin. He was talking with Coretta. "I've insisted that each member of our church registers as a voter and becomes a member of the NAACP."

"You're doing well, Martin." Coretta said.

"Now I've finished my studies I can turn to politics. I'm going to work with the NAACP myself."

Soon Martin was taking part in more NAACP activities and in time was elected one of the leaders of the Montgomery group. He was also involved with another action group called the Alabama Council on Human Relations. This interracial group sought integration through education.

In November 1955 Martin and Coretta finally had the child that they had longed for.

"What a whopper," exclaimed Martin, as he held his little girl for the first time.

"She's certainly a handful," whispered Coretta. The little handful was called Yolanda Denise. Now Martin had something other than thinking about the race issue to keep him up at night.

"Now, more than ever, I have to do something about the situation," he told Coretta. "I want our little girl to live in a society where she can go where she likes. I dream of her being anything she wants to be…"

Chapter Seven

"No, I won't get up," said Mrs Rosa Parks, quietly yet firmly as she stayed rooted in her seat in the unreserved section of the bus. Rosa was one of the trustiest old stalwarts of Montgomery Negro society. She worked hard as a tailor's assistant in a downtown store and did her bit for the NAACP, too.

"You know the rules, lady," the bus operator went on. "This man here needs your seat."

Rosa looked up at the white man who hovered in the aisle. She was fed up with this kind of treatment. Her feet were hurting her after a day at work and doing the shopping. It just didn't seem right that this man should have her seat.

"If you don't move, I'm going to have to call the police," the driver was getting impatient now.

"Then call the police," huffed Rosa. By now she was dead set on not budging. "Go ahead, have me arrested."

The first that Martin heard of Mrs Parks's arrest was a phone call on the morning of 2 December, 1955, from E.D. Nixon, another leader of the Montgomery NAACP.

"You will not believe what I'm about to tell you," Nixon began.

"No, go on," answered Martin.

Nixon went on to explain. Mrs Rosa Parks had been charged with violating the city segregation laws. Martin could sense Nixon's fury but he could also detect excitement creeping into the older man's voice.

"We have taken this kind of thing for too long," Nixon went on. "The time has come to boycott the buses. It's the only way to show the white people in this town that we will not tolerate this treatment."

Martin listened calmly to everything Nixon said and agreed that they needed to take some kind of action.

"Let's call a meeting." Nixon was fired up. "We'll get all the ministers and civil leaders we can together and make a plan."

"In that case I think we should meet at Dexter tonight," suggested Martin.

"This could be our moment, Martin," Nixon said before he put down the phone.

That night a crowd of about 50 people gathered at Dexter Baptist Church. They agreed to distribute 7000 leaflets urging the Negro community to boycott the buses on 5 December. That night the leaders also discussed the possibility of the case going to the Supreme Court. This could be the test case they were waiting for. If segregation on Montgomery's buses was ruled unlawful then it could set the ball rolling for all sorts of other cases against segregation.

***

It was dawn on 5 December, 1955. Martin had

hardly slept a wink. Now he sat with his hands clamped around his steaming coffee cup. Coretta was cuddling Yoki. It looked like the perfect domestic scene but the air was filled with expectation.

"I can hardly bring myself to look, Corrie," Martin raised his tired eyes to his wife. "Do you think they'll carry it through?"

"The first bus is due any moment," said Coretta. "I'll go to the window and tell you."

The minutes seemed to stretch while Coretta kept guard at the window.

"Martin, Martin, come and see!" Her face was lit up with delight. Martin leapt to the window.

"It's empty," he gushed. "There's nobody on that bus. It's normally packed with workers."

For the next hour Martin and Coretta stationed themselves at the window watching the buses pull up in front of their house. Except for a few white passengers, the buses were empty.

Martin shared his joy with fellow NAACP member Ralph Abernathy. Later that morning the two men drove around Montgomery to see if the boycott had worked throughout the town.

"This is wonderful," Martin's face hurt because he was grinning so hard. Everywhere they looked, the buses were empty. Instead the streets were filled with people walking to work. Some of them had walked miles but they were laughing and smiling. Many of them were old people but somehow they found the will to pick up their tired, old feet and join the protest.

"It's like a miracle," Martin shouted out.

That afternoon Martin was at City Hall attending Mrs Parks's trial. She was found guilty of breaking Montgomery's segregation laws and fined fourteen dollars.

"This is it," Martin's eyes twinkled as he looked at Ralph. "This case is going all the way to the Supreme Court."

Later that day the boycott leaders met once again. They formed the Montgomery Improvement Association (MIA) and appointed Martin as its president. That evening Martin gave his first political speech to the body of people who'd gathered at Holt Street Baptist Church: "As we stand and sit here this evening and as we prepare ourselves for what lies ahead, let us go out with a grim and bold determination that we are going to stick together."

The MIA decided that the protest should go on until all passengers were treated with respect. Black people would not tolerate being called "black cows", "niggers" or "black apes" any longer. The MIA also stated that the boycott would carry on until all passengers were seated on a first-come, first-served basis.

"We're standing for justice," Martin told the protesters. "This is not a war between the white and the Negro but a conflict between justice and injustice."

The black people of Montgomery did stick together. White people in the town who thought the protest would blow over were soon proved wrong. People were using old ponies and traps and bicycles to get about town. The MIA had also organized a car pool. January came and the weather turned bitterly cold but people dressed up warmly and walked to work or school. By now the boycott was crippling the local bus company and shops. Businesses were suffering. The white community looked for scapegoats.

Doctor Martin Luther King, the suave, well-spoken leader of the MIA certainly stood out as a troublemaker. Soon he was receiving death threats over the telephone.

"It was to be expected," Martin tried to sooth Coretta who felt worried about her husband's safety.

"Oh no, not this," said Coretta a few days later when her husband was arrested and imprisoned for going five mph over the speed limit. "I can't believe they've put him in jail for that."

Martin was freed without charge but a few days later things became much more scary.

***

On the evening of 30 January, 1956, a bomb was thrown onto the porch of Martin's home. At the time Martin was attending evening mass but Coretta and baby Yoki were at home. On the short journey back to his house Martin could hardly breath. As he approached his house he saw a mass of people. In the crowd were black and white people shouting abuse at each other.

Martin passed through the angry mob in a haze.

"Coretta, where are you?" he cried as he burst in through the front door.

"We're here darling," Martin felt his heart leap. Coretta and Yoki were in the bedroom.

"It's OK," Coretta was calm. "But I don't like the sound of that crowd outside."

Martin looked out the window and saw policemen had joined in the fracas. This thing was getting bigger than he'd expected. Tentatively, he returned to the porch to address the crowd.

"Don't get your weapons," he told them. "He who lives by the sword will perish by the sword. Remember that is what God said. We are not advocating violence. We want to love our enemies."

Somehow Martin's words worked their magic on the crowd and it broke up without causing any trouble. Later, as Martin lay in bed he tried to come to terms with what had happened. The fight was beginning to get nasty. Suddenly what was going on in Montgomery seemed much bigger. Even so, everything became much clearer in his head. This was what he was needed for – this was his calling. As Martin played with these thoughts he felt a chill deep inside. This was dangerous work. There were people out there who wanted to kill him. And, there were policemen who wanted to find any excuse to arrest him. With the odds against him, was he strong enough to face the challenge ahead?

Chapter eight

The brave people of Montgomery rose to their challenge. The Montgomery Bus Boycott lasted nearly a year. Then, in November 1956, the Supreme Court ruled that bus segregation in Alabama was unconstitutional. In the course of that year Martin withstood more threats and was arrested and fined for leading the protest movement. He never ever doubted he was doing the right thing, though. Nor did the thousands of black people in America who wrote to him, congratulating him on his work.

"This is an historic moment, Rosa!" Martin told Mrs Parks as they took their seats on the first integrated bus ride in Montgomery. It was 20 December, 1956. Rosa Parks sat beside Ralph Abernathy while Martin occupied the seat behind them, next to Reverend Glenn Smiley, a Southern-born white minister.

"Do you know what really surprises me?" Martin looked genuinely pleased as he saw black and white people sitting together. "Most of the white folk have just accepted integration. It gives me great hope."

Martin's great hope was soon dashed. A few days later the Ku Klux Klan began another terror campaign in Montgomery. Once again the night skies were lit up with their ominous crosses of fire. Then, in January 1957, four black churches and two parsonages were bombed. Martin was devastated that people would attack religious institutions. That same month, the Southern Leaders Conference (SCLC) was formed, with Martin as its president. At one of its first meetings Martin addressed the crowd.

"Lord, I hope no one will have to die as a result of our struggle for freedom in Montgomery," his voice was choked with emotion. "But if anyone has to die, let it be me."

By now Martin had become a celebrity. He appeared on television, and newspaper journalists flocked to Montgomery to interview the charismatic leader of the SCLC. In February 1957 Martin was featured on the cover of *Time* magazine. In the leading article the journalist wrote: "Martin Luther King Jr. is, in fact, what many a Negro – and, were it not for his color [sic], many a white – would like to be." To many people Martin had become the spokesman for all Negroes in the US.

In private, Martin had misgivings about his new hero status. He was just 27 years old. In some ways he worried that he might have hit his peak early and that he had nothing left to give.

"This has all happened so quickly," he told Coretta. "People are beginning to think that I can perform miracles. I don't want to disappoint… There is just so much work to be done."

"Don't let the pressure get to you, darling," Coretta looked concerned.

"Some people think that segregation will be scrapped by 1963," Martin rubbed his tired eyes. "Can't they see how unrealistic that is? It's more likely to be the year 2000!"

On 17 May, 1957, Martin lead a Prayer Pilgrimage to Washington, DC. The date was the third anniversary of the Supreme Court's decision outlawing segregation in schools. A crowd of about 25,000 people gathered before the Lincoln Memorial in the city.

"I had hoped for a crowd of nearer 70,000," Martin told Ralph Abernathy before he stepped up to the roster to address the crowd.

"Don't be disappointed," Ralph patted Martin's back. "We'll do this, one step at a time."

***

Martin was the last speaker that day and he made an urgent request to President Eisenhower to give Negroes the right to vote throughout the South:

"Give us the ballot and we will no longer have to worry the federal government about our basic rights," he pleaded in his deep, melodic voice.

"Give us the ballot and we will transform the salient misdeeds of bloodthirsty mobs into the calculated good deeds of orderly citizens…" As he repeated each demand Martin raised his arms. Such was his fervour and passion he could easily have been standing behind the pulpit delivering a sermon. As he said each line the crowd clapped and cheered in agreement. It was a powerful way of moving the people. And, as Martin stepped down from the roster, he felt the wave of optimism hit him again.

"It's going to be OK," he told Ralph.

"I know," agreed Ralph, who never doubted Martin for a moment.

It also moved the government. In September 1957 a Civil Rights act was pushed through Congress by Senator Lyndon B. Johnson. Martin was disappointed with the act.

"It isn't enough," he told Ralph. "All they have done is set up the Civil Rights Commission. All that does is investigate charges of people not being able to vote."

"It's a start," reasoned Ralph. "This is the first Civil Rights legislation for decades."

"But, it doesn't change the everyday lives of ordinary people." Martin looked deflated.

***

Elizabeth Eckford was just an ordinary girl. She was fifteen years old and dreamed of getting to college. In Little Rock, Arkansas, that wasn't easy for a black girl.

"Now that the federal court has ordered the Central High School to admit Negro students I reckon I've got as good a chance as anyone," Elizabeth told her mother on a September morning in 1957 – the day that she was about to begin at her new school. She felt nervous and excited at the same time. Excited, because at last she could get on with her education. But she was nervous because she knew that many of the white pupils would taunt her for being black. Even though the law said she was allowed to go to their school, many white pupils didn't want her there.

"I know you're going to do well, honey." Mrs Eckford felt anxious.

She was so proud of her daughter and her quest for achievement. But, boy oh boy, she knew the risks involved. When they were whipped up, the white people of Little Rock could be mighty cruel.

"Thanks Mama," Elizabeth reached up and kissed her mother, "I'm going to be fine."

When Elizabeth got to the school gate her eyes widened with shock.

"Go home, nigger. You ain't welcome at this school," jeered a man. His face was puffed up and red like an overripe tomato. Around him an angry mass of white parents thumped the air and cheered in agreement.

"Go home! Go home!" they yelled.

Elizabeth's brisk step slowed down. Alongside the spitting mob, there were soldiers carrying guns. Guns! Elizabeth couldn't believe her eyes. She tried to stop the trembling inside. Her tongue felt as dry as a duster in the roof of her mouth. She clutched her school bag close to her chest. She simply didn't know what to say. Slowly, she began backing away.

"That's right girl, go back to where you belong," the red-faced man shouted. On shaky legs, Elizabeth made her way to the bus stop. But she wasn't safe there either. The mob followed her, shouting and spitting more of their angry bile.

A few days later Elizabeth returned to the school. This time she had friends with her. Even so, it took every bit of Elizabeth's courage to go back to the school. She was stunned when the same white folk gathered and spewed out their vicious poison.

"Go home niggers," they chanted.

The situation got so out of hand that President Eisenhower eventually sent one thousand US paratroopers to Little Rock to escort Elizabeth and eight of her friends to school.

***

"Can you believe it?" boomed Martin at the breakfast table. "Those kids had to be escorted to the classroom by armed federal troops!"

Coretta tried to keep her cool. She was heavily pregnant and didn't need to be rattled at the moment. Martin looked across at his daughter Yoki.

"To think they treated a young girl like that; it makes my blood boil."

"I know, honey," soothed Coretta as she smoothed a hand over her large belly.

"I never ever want that for my children."

That October, Coretta gave birth to little Martin Luther King III. He was just one more reason for Martin to carry on with the cause.

Chapter Nine

Sometimes Martin felt his life wasn't his own. "And it certainly isn't my family's, as it should be," he confided in Ralph.

"I know," agreed Ralph. "If it isn't meetings, it's public appearances. Everyone wants to hear you speak."

"And, then there's my job at Dexter, my congregation needs me too," Martin look tired. When he did catch a spare moment, he used it to write his book about the Montgomery bus boycott.

"Sometimes, I wonder how I'm going to keep going," Martin sighed heavily.

But Martin did keep going. In February 1958, the SCLC launched the Crusade for Citizenship. The aim of this campaign was to get two million black people to register for the vote before the 1960 presidential election. Later that summer his book *Stride Toward Freedom* also hit the bookshops. Martin now added television and radio appearances to his already hectic schedule.

"I have these awful dreams," Coretta told one of her friends. "I keep dreaming that someone is going to kill Martin."

"You're just over-tired Coretta," her friend replied, "He's going to be fine. Everyone loves Martin. He's their hero."

"But these dreams are so real," insisted Coretta. "I just worry all the time."

***

That September Martin was in New York, attending a book signing at Blumstein's, one of the city's major department stores. Martin sat behind a table mounded with his books. Behind the pile there was a sea of black and white faces queuing to meet him. That felt good...

"Are you Martin Luther King?" Martin didn't a get chance to look up at the smartly dressed black woman who'd approached the table. No sooner had he said "Yes," then he felt something touch his chest.

"Luther King," the woman shrilly cried, "I've been after you for five years."

Martin looked up in disbelief as the woman plunged a letter opener into him. Next the woman bolted. Martin looked down and saw that the blade was near his heart. He felt sure he was dying, and yet strangely he didn't feel any pain. Instead, he thought about Corrie... and the children...

***

Martin was rushed to Harlem Hospital and operated upon immediately.

"You're one lucky man," the surgeon told Martin afterwards. "One sneeze and that blade could have severed your major artery. You'd have drowned in your own blood."

Martin was too foggy to respond. Later he heard how the surgeon had removed one of his ribs and part of his breastbone to get the blade out. Coretta flew from Montgomery to be at her husband's bedside.

"You must rest and get better," she told him firmly. And for once, Martin did as he was told.

It took Martin nearly a month to recover. In that time he asked himself why this terrible thing had happened. He also thought about Izola Curry, the woman who had nearly killed him. It turned out she was from a broken home and was divorced. She was rootless and probably mentally ill.

"I don't want her to be charged," Martin insisted. "That woman needs help."

"Mrs Curry nearly killed me," he told Coretta "but I'm still here. God obviously wants me to continue with my work."

Chapter Ten

"Goodbye Dexter, I shall miss you." Martin felt a lump in his throat as he walked out of the redbrick church for the last time as its pastor. It was the end of January 1960. A few days earlier he'd given his final sermon. There had been tears all round. The congregation had wept. Martin had bitten back the tears as he told them he was going.

"History has thrust upon me a responsibility from which I cannot turn away," he said. "I have no choice but to free you."

Now Martin was saying his own quiet farewell to the little church. As the heavy door swung closed behind him he felt like the next chapter of his life was ready to begin.

***

In Atlanta, Martin became co-pastor of his father's church, the Ebenezer Baptist Church. The family was just settling in to their new life and new home, a rented house on Johnson Avenue, when an exciting development took place in the Civil Rights movement.

"Look, darling," Martin pushed the newspaper over to Coretta to see. "Those kids are brilliant. What an inspiration!" Martin's face was flushed with excitement.

Coretta scanned the story. It was about four Negro students from North Carolina A & T College who had walked into the local Woolworth's and sat down at the segregated lunch counter. They had flat refused to move when they were told to get up. Instead, they had demanded to be served. Of course, they weren't served. The police were called and the students had to be removed by force. The students had remained peaceful throughout the protest. And, even though they were moved on that day, they came back to protest the next day.

"Wow," Coretta felt a tingle of excitement too. "That's really something."

Within days many more students were occupying Woolworth's lunch counters. By staging these sit-ins they hoped to get themselves arrested. Eventually, the prisons would be so full up that the government would have to cave in to their demands for desegregated lunch counters. As the weeks passed similar sit-ins were happening throughout the Southern states.

"I've been asked to join the students at some of the sit-ins," Martin told Coretta.

"I'm so pleased that they are doing something positive," Coretta went on, "but you don't have time, darling."

"It's not just that," Martin looked torn. "This is *their* thing. You know I support what they're doing but at the same time this is something that the young people need to do for themselves."

While the students stepped up their struggle,

Martin worried about the future of the Civil Rights movement as a whole. The SCLC needed much more money. Meanwhile, there was a presidential election set for November 1960… And so much to do before then…

***

That June, Martin met with John F. Kennedy, the charismatic candidate for the Democratic party. Martin looked across the breakfast table at Kennedy. The young man – well, at 43 he was considerably younger than any president of the United States had ever been – was certainly slick. He looked more like a movie star than a politician. And, when he smiled, his whole face lit up like a toothpaste advertisement. Ah, thought Martin cautiously, but could he be trusted to help the cause? What were his thoughts on segregation? What would he do for Negroes?

"Would you be prepared to endorse the sit-ins?" Martin asked Kennedy.

"We certainly favour desegregation," Kennedy replied, giving very little away. "You tell us what it is you want, and our administration will try its best."

Martin realized that Kennedy needed him on his side. Kennedy needed the black vote if he were to win the presidential election. For that reason, Martin didn't offer Kennedy the support he obviously wanted — yet. He could afford to be cautious. There were still some months to go before the election and Martin meant to keep a watchful eye on the campaign before supporting anybody.

"It's been a great pleasure meeting you, Mr King," Kennedy gave Martin a firm handshake as they said their goodbyes.

"Likewise, Mr Kennedy." And Martin meant it; he thought the presidential candidate seemed honest and forthright. Perhaps he would be somebody he could do business with.

In October 1960, Martin finally joined the students on one of their sit-ins.

"Do you know how much it means to have you with us today?" One of the female protesters looked up at him with adoration in her eyes.

"You are the spiritual leader of the movement," said another student, equally delighted to have the great Mr King on their side.

That day Martin and about 75 students were piling into Rich's snack bar.

"You know the drill," shouted one of the leaders of the protest.

"Get in there, and sit down!"

Martin was enjoying himself. Around him he could see students with fire in their eyes. This is what it was like to be at the frontline. As the mob took over the snack bar there was a look of resignation on the faces of the cooks and waiting staff. These sit-ins had been well publicised and they knew what was coming. First, there'd be a great big kerfuffle. Next there'd be a bout of singing. Then, ker pow! – the cops would show up. With that, the students began to sing.

"*We shall overcome, we shall overcome,*" they sang. Martin linked hands with the students nearest to him and joined in. It was an old Negro spiritual hymn and it meant a lot to him.

"*Oh, deep in my heart I do believe, that we shall overcome some day...*" he bellowed. And, he knew what was coming. He'd be arrested and if he refused to pay the fine then he'd be thrown in jail. He had every intention of not paying the fine.

Later that night Martin found himself in a cell with many of the other students.

"So what was it like to be at Montgomery during the boycott?" asked one of the young men in the nearby bunks.

"It was wonderful to see what ordinary people can do. To protest peacefully is the most powerful tool we have." Martin explained.

"When white people hurt us, don't you think we should fight back?" the young man looked puzzled.

"No, I don't think violence is ever the way," Martin replied and tried to settle down to sleep for the night.

A few days later the students were released. Apparently Senator John F. Kennedy had asked the local mayor to free the students. If the students agreed to put a stop to the sit-ins then negotiations could take place with the owners of the local lunch counters. Perhaps these talks would lead to desegregation. Martin thought he'd go free too but instead he was handed over to a prison in another county. They claimed he should stand trial for a previous traffic offence. It was a minor offence but the authorities were out to get Martin Luther King.

On October 25, Martin was found guilty and sentenced to four months in one of Georgia's notorious hard labour work camps.

"People go in there," wailed Coretta, "and they never come out again. I don't see how he's gonna face it."

Daddy King tried to comfort her but this time Coretta's tears fell like heavy showers.

"He told me he'll be OK if I take him books and paper, but what can books and paper do for him when he's surrounded by brutes who want to kill him?"

"Trust in him, Coretta. He's tougher than you know."

It took every bit of Coretta's faith to get through the next few days. While she fretted, her husband awaited his fate in a damp cell. At night, cockroaches crawled out of the cracks and flitted across the floor. As the temperature dropped Martin huddled into himself to keep warm. He felt scared... Would he ever see his family again?

Three days later Martin was released from jail. On

the way home Martin couldn't stop thinking. Who had secured his release? Who had pulled the strings? Later that day Coretta told Martin how Senator Kennedy had helped him.

"Kennedy rang me up, darling," explained Coretta. "He promised to help in every way he could. Then, what do you know, he goes and gets you released!"

"Wow," Martin was amazed.

"That's it," boomed Daddy King, "that man is getting my vote."

***

"And mine," said many thousands of Negroes who had heard about how Kennedy had helped get Martin Luther King out of jail. That November Kennedy was elected president. He'd walked away with nearly three quarters of the Negro vote.

"At last," Martin said in private, "Here is somebody who will help us."

Chapter eleven

"Ask not what your country can do for you but what you can do for your country."

These famous words were spoken by President J. F. Kennedy in his inauguration speech of January 1961. The bright young President brought with him hope and confidence for a better America. His optimism reached far and wide, touching those who were fighting for Civil Rights. That same month Martin and Coretta welcomed their third child into the world, a son they named Dexter.

The spring of 1961 also brought another form of demonstration. Groups of black and white people were boarding buses going South and purposely using the segregated facilities en route. Simply by using white-only toilets or occupying the lunch-counters they hoped to change the law. These protests were called Freedom Rides.

***

Martin was angry. He'd seen photographs of the bus set alight in Alabama. The Freedom Riders had only just escaped before the bus exploded. Apparently, the Klan was behind that. Now Martin was pacing his living room as he watched the television. The wonder of modern science meant that he could view real-life violence and bloodshed in the shelter of his own home. And so it was that he watched in horror as a bus pulled up into the Montgomery bus station. At first everything was quiet – too quiet, the silence before a storm. Then, suddenly, there was a stampede of white men brandishing clubs, metal pipes and chains. Their arms were raised and they were shouting "Kill the niggers, kill the nigger-loving sons-of-bitches!"

Martin felt his insides shrink as he saw this wall of hate bash their weapons on the defenseless Freedom Riders.

"I'll be in Montgomery later today," Martin barked down the phone to Ralph Abernathy. "I'm going to stand in line with those students."

Within hours President Kennedy's brother Robert, also a politician, was on the phone to Martin.

"You can't go there," he pleaded. "It simply isn't safe. I can't protect you."

"I have to go," Martin could not be dissuaded – even when his wife looked at him with her big, sorrowful eyes, silently begging him not to go. Not even when little Yoki put her arms around his legs and begged, "Don't go Daddy!"

The words of his little girl came back to Martin later that night when he was barricaded into Ralph Abernathy's church. Martin had rushed to Montgomery and spoken in support of the Freedom Riders. As he delivered his speech the vile words of a mob outside filtered into the church. Then suddenly, it was hell in heaven's sanctuary as a car outside was set on fire and the mob began to attack the church. Martin's eyes were wide with fear as the first of many rocks rained in through the beautiful stained-glass windows. People lay on the floor amongst the shattered glass. Then, there was the tear gas. Somehow, despite the panic, Martin managed to get to a phone to call Robert Kennedy.

"They're about to burn the place down to the ground," he shouted down the receiver. "You've got to help us."

"Soldiers are on their way," Kennedy assured him.

Outside the church, federal marshals had arrived to confront the mob. The battle continued for hours by which time the state police had joined in. When it finally ended, Martin stepped over the broken glass and made his way outside the church. They were still alive. Ready to fight the cause another day.

***

In the summer of 1961, 400 Freedom Riders were arrested and three of them were killed. Robert Kennedy urged Martin to stop the Freedom Rides for the safety of the participants, but he refused. Meanwhile, Martin hoped that President Kennedy would pass new regulations banning segregation on transport and in stations. After a long hard battle, the Freedom Riders won their desegregated stations.

By the end of the year, Martin had plunged himself into his next campaign in Albany, Georgia. A series of marches and sit-ins were staged to end segregation in the city. Once again Martin was arrested and imprisoned but this time no changes were made to the Constitution. Martin was depressed with the lack of progress, and resolved to work all the harder on his next project.

In 1963, the SCLC launched a new Civil Rights campaign in Birmingham, Alabama. If anywhere needed to be desegregated it was the industrial city of Birmingham. It was with great sadness that Martin wrote about the place: "It was a community in which human rights had been trampled on for so long that fear and oppression were as thick in its atmosphere as the smog from its factories." The SCLC drew up the Birmingham Manifesto to include demands for desegregation and more jobs for Negroes. That

April a series of boycotts, sit-ins and marches began. After just ten days of demonstrations, hundreds of people had been jailed.

On 12 April, Good Friday, Martin and his good friend Ralph Abernathy, took their places in a peaceful march through downtown Birmingham.

"This is surely a beautiful march," said Martin as he took in the sunshine and the faces of other protesters.

"People are actually applauding us, see," answered Ralph, gesturing to the people on the sidewalks who were clapping them.

"I don't know what's going to happen," Martin looked strangely relaxed. "But I'm putting my faith in God."

As the marchers proceeded slowly through the streets, they were singing hymns. Martin loved to sing. In the face of despair, music had always brought hope to Negroes. It was while he was singing that Martin felt a police officer grab the back of his shirt. Then he was hauled off to Birmingham jail.

Martin was placed in solitary confinement. While he was there he saw an article written by white religious leaders urging Martin and the SCLC to end their protests. Martin was compelled to write back: "For years now I have heard the word 'Wait!' It rings in the ears of every Negro with piercing familiarity. This 'Wait' has almost always meant 'Never'."

After eight days Martin was released. He was more determined than ever to continue with the campaign. That was when the SCLC called upon the children of Birmingham to join the protest. On 2 May, 1963, more than a thousand children marched into Birmingham. By the end of the day, 900 youngsters had been arrested and put in jail. Martin was delighted because it showed the determination of the young. The next day 2,500 children marched into Birmingham. Nobody was prepared for the scenes that followed.

***

"Quick," shouted Alice. "Hide behind here."

Alice looked all around her, trying to find her sister. The last time she remembered seeing her was when the police opened the fire hoses. Somehow Alice had clambered behind a pile of garbage to escape the punishing jet of water. Where was Anna? Alice could hear screaming. Fierce, frightened, blood-curdling screams — was that Anna? Alice felt lightheaded as her heart began to pound furiously.

"Mama," wailed Charlie. "Help me, Mama."

Charlie was twelve years old. This morning he'd felt like a man as he'd set off on the march. Then the jets of water had thrown him to the floor. Now, he hurt all over. But what pained him most of all was that this day of hope had been ruined. Now all he wanted was the warm arms of his mother.

"Police dogs!" screamed the white woman who'd been watching the march. "How can you animals set dogs on children? Stop this, stop this…"

Her voice became hoarse as her pleas fell on deaf ears. She simply couldn't believe what she was seeing. The police were using dogs and cattle prods on the children. This was America — this sort of thing didn't happen here.

The next day, the world stood back in disbelief. Television cameras had captured the horror of events in Birmingham. America hung its head in shame. The local politicians had no choice but to give in to desegregation and other demands. But, there was more trouble ahead. After the agreement, the streets of Birmingham remained heavy with tension. Violence between blacks and whites flared. Then, the hotel in which Martin had been staying was bombed.

"That was meant for me," said Martin. By this time he was back in Atlanta, far away from the troubles.

After the bomb, came the riots – the black community were fighting back. Martin pleaded with President Kennedy to send in troops. Kennedy brought in federal soldiers. Then, on 11 June, the president appeared on national television and delivered a speech in which he proposed a new Civil Rights bill.

"At last," murmured Martin. "At last…"

Chapter Twelve

Martin spent the summer of 1963 touring the USA, drumming up support for the great 'March on Washington for Jobs and Freedom'. When the day of the march finally dawned on 28 August, Martin was pacing the floor of his suite at the Willard Hotel.

"Did you get any sleep?" asked Ralph.

"Not much. I kept going over my speech." Martin gestured to the pieces of paper in his hands. "I've only got eight minutes to talk. It has to be something really special, Ralph."

This was true. Today he needed to appeal to

everyone if the Civil Rights Bill were to sail through Congress.

"Uh huh," Ralph agreed, "Millions of people will be watching on television, too. This is sure going to be a big day."

"What are the crowds out there like, Ralph? I hardly dare look."

"There are already plenty of people heading to the Memorial," answered Ralph as he peered out of the window. "News reports say there'll be about 25,000."

"That's disappointing isn't it... Let's pray for more," said Martin.

***

When Coretta awoke she found Martin at the window.

"Come and look darling," Martin pulled her to his side. "Just look at them."

Below them they could see thousands of people enjoying the morning sunshine as they made their way into town. Many of them had placards saying where they were from. If they were not chatting and laughing, then they were singing songs. The atmosphere was joyful.

"Many of them have come from the South. They've driven here in specially chartered buses." Martin said.

"There are some real poor people down there," Coretta smiled down on the crowd. "But, just look at them in their neatly pressed clothes. It makes me so proud."

"There's going to be an enormous turnout – I just know it," Martin said with an excited glint in his eyes.

That day an estimated 250,000 people gathered on the lawns and streets surrounding the White House and the Lincoln Memorial, making it the biggest ever Civil Rights demonstration in US history. In that crowd were people of every race, age and political persuasion. There were also film stars such as Sidney Poitier, Marlon Brando, Harry Belafonte, Charlton Heston and Burt Lancaster. The singers Sammy Davis Jr and Judy Garland also put in an appearance.

"Bring on the Doctor," yelled a man in the crowd.

"We want the Doctor," echoed the crowd. By 3.00pm, after about three hours of speeches and introductions, everyone was beginning to feel restless and impatient to hear Martin Luther King give his speech.

"I can't wait to hear him," whispered a young girl as Martin took the podium, "This is the moment I've been waiting for."

Now all eyes were on Martin. He felt trickles of sweat pour down his back – that was the heat as well as his nerves.

"Five score years ago a great American, in whose symbolic shadow we stand today, signed the Emancipation Proclamation," he began. The crowd was silent, drinking in his fine words spoken in that reassuring deep voice.

"This momentous decree came as a great beacon light of hope to millions of Negro slaves who had been seared in the flames of withering injustice… But one hundred years later, the Negro still is not free."

The crowd cheered in agreement. All of a sudden, Martin felt something lift inside him. Now all those words he'd spent a lifetime gathering were going to be let free. And here was an audience who couldn't wait to hear those words.

Martin's speech ran over his allotted time — to more than nineteen minutes. It was a long time to keep a crowd engaged but the beauty of his words and the hope they brought kept the crowd enraptured. And there was one part of his speech that cast the most magical spell over everyone.

"*I have a dream...*" he told the crowd and went on to reveal his hopes and dreams of a free America.

"*I have a dream* that one day on the red hills of Georgia the sons of former slaves and the sons of former slave owners will be able to sit down together at the table of brotherhood."

The crowd listened, awestruck.

"*I have a dream* that one day even the state of Mississippi, a desert state sweltering with the heat of injustice and oppression, will be transformed into an oasis of freedom and justice."

He continued with his refrain and towards the end of the speech he called for freedom throughout America.

"Let freedom ring from the snowcapped Rockies of Colorado!" he pleaded. "Let freedom ring from every hill and molehill of Mississippi. From every mountainside, let freedom ring."

By now the crowd were whooping and cheering in agreement. As they looked towards the stage they saw Martin on tiptoe with his arms in the air as if he were reaching towards Heaven.

"When we let freedom ring, when we let it ring from every village and every hamlet, from every state and every city, we will be able to speed up that day when all of God's children, black men and white men, Jews and Gentiles, Protestants and Catholics, will be able to join hands and sing in the words of the Old Negro spiritual, '*Free at last! Free at last! Thank God almighty, we are free at last!*'"

In the moments after the speech there was total silence. People were lost in their own thoughts as they absorbed Martin's words. As they craned their eyes to the White House, they hoped that President Kennedy was as moved as they were. Surely, the Civil Rights Bill would be passed through Congress now.

As the crowd filtered away, Martin and the other leaders of the SCLC made their way to the White House to meet the President.

"I have a dream…" were President Kennedy's

opening words to Martin as he reached to shake his hand.

"Thank you," said Martin who was pleased the President had picked up on that particular line.

"Now we just need to get that bill through, and I want you to know you have my full support." Kennedy beamed brightly.

***

Two weeks later it felt like that marvellous day with all its optimism and hope had never happened.

"I can't believe it," Martin held his face in his hands. He'd just finished a sermon at his father's church. He had been feeling on top of the world. Then this. "How could they bomb a church?"

Ralph went on to tell him how the Sixteenth Street Baptist Church in Birmingham had been attacked that very morning.

"You mean, while I was preaching loving the enemy to my congregation over here in Atlanta, they were killing worshippers over in Birmingham?"

Ralph nodded gravely. "Four young girls were

killed," Ralph added.

This knowledge seemed to tear at Martin's insides.

"If men are this evil then is there any hope?"

It was a question Martin asked himself again a few months later, on 22 November, 1963. For, on that day President John F. Kennedy was shot and killed in Dallas, Texas. When Martin heard the news he was at home with his family.

"I don't think I'm going to live to reach forty." Martin looked grief-stricken. If somebody could shoot the President, then they could shoot him, too.

"Please don't say that," Coretta asked him.

"Daddy, President Kennedy was your best friend wasn't he?" asked Marty in a quiet voice.

"As good as," said Martin, as he hugged his little boy close to him.

"That poor, poor man," Coretta tried to hold back her tears.

"What a terrible loss," Martin said. "I'll miss him so much. And so will America."

Chapter thirteen

These became dark days in American history. People mourned the loss of President John F. Kennedy. Many people also questioned what had been achieved in the Civil Rights movement. Would the new president, President Lyndon Johnson stand by the Civil Rights protesters? Kennedy's Civil Rights bill was yet to be passed through Congress. Fortunately, President Johnson made sure that it was passed.

On 2 July, 1964, Martin Luther King attended the signing of the Civil Rights Act. Then, in October 1964, he was awarded the Nobel Peace Prize. At 35 years old, he was the youngest man ever to win the precious award. In his acceptance speech in Oslo, Norway, he said: "We have learned to fly the air like birds and even swim the sea like fish, but we have not learned the simple arts of living together like brothers…"

***

Late one night, Coretta walked in on her husband as he was sifting through mounds of paperwork. In his hand was the pen that President Johnson had used to sign the Civil Rights Act.

"This is one of my most cherished possessions," he told her.

"It was very kind of the President to give it to you," Coretta said.

"It means so much, my dear," he looked at her with his tired eyes. "This has been a terrific year. But, there is still so much to do."

"I wish you'd slow down, Martin," Coretta sighed. "I worry about you."

"I worry about America," Martin continued.

"Everywhere in this country I see black people living in poverty. They've been promised change but they still get the worst jobs. In Mississippi there are people who've been promised the vote, but they still don't get to the ballot box."

"Martin, you're doing everything you can. You support them all. You go on the marches. You mastermind the protests. You're fighting for the vote."

"Yes, but it's getting harder. It's getting more violent. The young people want change now. They're impatient and there's going to be big trouble."

And trouble did erupt, in 1965. In January, Martin was attacked in Selma, Alabama, while he was campaigning for voter registration. Then in February, Malcolm X, the young black Muslim leader, was assassinated. He had different ideas to Martin about the struggle for Civil Rights. To begin with, anyway, he told black people to fight back, using violence if necessary. Meanwhile, America sent more troops to fight the war in Vietnam. Many people were against America's involvement in the war. Martin spoke out against the war, too, and tried to sway the President in favour of peace.

In March there was good news for the Civil Rights movement. President Johnson announced the Voting Rights Act of 1965. But, in August 1965 all hell broke loose in Watts, a black suburb of Los Angeles. Riots flared, homes were set alight by a mob of angry black men. The streets were alive with the cries of "Burn, baby, burn!" Eventually the national guard was called in. It was too late. In a matter of days, 34 people were killed and 850 people were injured. Over 200 buildings had been burned down. Some people blamed the police for being too heavy-handed. Others claimed the hot weather had sent people berserk.

Martin rushed to Watts to see what he could do.

"We won," said one of the young men that Martin talked with on the burning streets.

"What do you mean, 'we won'? Thirty-some people dead – all but two are Negroes! You've destroyed your own. What do you mean?" Martin was horrified.

"*We* made them pay attention to us, didn't we?" answered the young man with a look of triumph on his face.

Martin was dismayed. These people had no other

way of being heard. Violence was their only answer. Martin hated violence but he realized it had been stirred by deprivation. What was worse, this would happen again if these people didn't get a better deal.

Chapter Fourteen

Throughout the mid-1960s, members of the black community turned to violence to make changes to the racial situation in America. A militant organization called the Black Panthers grew in strength. And, many ordinary people joined a new movement called Black Power. Young people were even claiming that Martin Luther King was out of touch with what was really happening. How could they win the war on Civil Rights with non-violent protest?

"We're moving to Chicago," Martin told Coretta in early 1966. "To fight against the poverty in the ghettoes we've got to be there ourselves. We've got to live amongst ordinary people who are struggling in the city."

Coretta was scared. They were going to live in an area called Lawndale. Basically, it was a slum. Chicago was a rich city but this black ghetto was filled with dark, dank houses and poor, snotty-nosed children. The kids were neglected by society and ignored by their own parents who worked too many hours for too little money.

"Even the rats attack the children in Lawnsdale," said Coretta. She dreaded taking her own children there.

***

"Do you think this was wise?" Coretta asked her husband one night soon after they'd moved to Lawndale. The children were in bed. It was a relief. They'd been playing up all day.

"It's not like the boys to explode like that," said Martin.

"This place is having a bad effect on them," Coretta agreed.

"Probably the heat," Martin said but didn't really believe it himself.

"It's hardly surprising," Coretta told him. "We're couped up in this small flat like pigs in a pen. The corridors smell of urine. There's no grass anywhere – just dirt and filth."

"I know," said Martin, "this place is dreadful. It's like an emotional pressure cooker round here. No wonder there's trouble in this city – it's always here, just bubbling up under the surface."

That July there were riots in Chicago. Martin had gone there to back a campaign on poverty and to help improve housing and employment for black people. Through non-violent marches and other protests some of the ghettoes were being cleaned up. The campaign had succeeded in getting fairer rents and more jobs for black people, too. Change was in the air but so was a simmering violence. Martin began to feel depressed about the situation. He took a break from the movement for a few months and wrote a book, called *Where Do We Go From Here?*

"I tell you where I want to go from here," said Coretta. "I want to go back to Atlanta."

Martin looked at his wife. It was the autumn of 1966. They'd spent a good six months in Chicago. Coretta looked drained. It was time to go back.

"I know honey," said Martin with feeling. "It's been very hard on you and the family. It's never been easy for you. I'm away from the family so often and you have to take charge of everything in the home. And I know there's never much money for all the things you'd like." This was true: even when Martin was given money for earning the Nobel Peace Prize he churned it back into the movement.

"I don't mind that, Martin," Coretta explained. "I just want our children out of this place."

"Yes, I know." Martin paused and pulled Coretta close to him. "Oh my, I hope I've been a good husband to you Coretta,"

"Hey you, don't talk like that," Coretta patted his back. "You're talking like you're leaving us or something…"

"I'd never do that," Martin replied. "Never!"

"So don't talk like it's the end," Coretta said, with a catch in her voice. "I simply won't have it."

***

It wasn't the end for Martin. There was still so much more to be done. The family moved back to Atlanta. He continued to speak out against the war in Vietnam and he finished another book. *Why We Can't Wait* was Martin's most radical work yet. He had new ideas about poverty. He believed the government should help black people and other disadvantaged people in society. In early 1967, Martin also began planning the "Poor People's Campaign".

"This is going to be the big one," Martin told Ralph Abernathy. "We're going to get better jobs and incomes for everyone."

"You should slow down Martin." Ralph was concerned for his friend. He'd been depressed for a long time now.

"There'll be an even bigger march on Washington this time," Martin said, with that old gleam in his eye.

"Your dream has never faded, has it?" Ralph said with meaning.

"No, if anything it's even bigger," Martin went on. "We'll keep making our demands until they hear us."

***

"Why are you going away again?" wailed Dexter, Martin's youngest son.

"It's my work," explained Martin. "I've got to go. They need me in Memphis. I'm going on a march with the refuse workers. We're going to get them fairer pay."

"I don't want you to go to Memphis," Dexter continued. "It just doesn't feel right. Yoki, Martin and me are scared for you, Daddy."

"Oh come on, Dexter, I'll be fine."

"I don't want you to go to jail again," Dexter said. Martin pulled his son to his chest and closed his eyes. If the truth be known he didn't want to go to jail again. But, this was his work. This was his life.

***

"Thank you for the flowers," Coretta told Martin. It was mid-March, 1968. Martin had been away to Memphis so many times this year. Sometimes he sent her flowers before he went away. And on this occasion she was delighted as ever to have been given flowers, but one thing puzzled her. Martin always, always sent her fresh flowers. This time, for some reason, he'd sent her artificial red carnations. They were beautiful – but it just didn't seem right that he'd sent her artificial flowers. The thought niggled Coretta.

"I hope you like them," said Martin.

"Oh yes," answered Coretta, "I just wondered why you chose artificial flowers?"

"I wanted to give you something that you could always keep," Martin told her. Coretta felt a strange chill.

***

On 28 March, 1968 Martin led a march of 6,000 refuse workers in Memphis.

"You know they have a great movement here," Martin told Ralph as they set off. The two men, friends for so many years now, headed the march. In that instant, they shared a knowing look. Nobody really knew how the march would go. These days everything was so unpredictable. Violence always seemed to be just a breath away.

"God help us," Martin said to himself as he moved forward.

The protest began peacefully. One moment they had been singing. The next there was the sound of breaking glass. A crowd of Black Power supporters began throwing rocks through shop windows. Then the police came and the riot began. Martin was whisked away under police escort. When he returned home his family threw themselves into his arms.

"Please don't go to Memphis again," begged Dexter.

Chapter Fifteen

"I'm scared, Ralph," said Martin. It was 3 April, 1968. They were flying to Memphis. That night Martin was going to speak, yet again, before a crowd of refuse workers.

"I'm always scared," joked Ralph, trying to lighten the atmosphere. Martin seemed so serious today.

"I don't know," Martin went on. "I've lived with the death threats ever since Montgomery. But, they're really beginning to frighten me now."

"Have faith, Martin," answered Ralph. "You've always had faith. And, you've given me and millions of others the strength to believe they can win."

That night Martin spoke in front of the refuse workers. When he was a little boy he talked about getting himself some "big words". Now the big words flowed from his lips.

"Well, I don't know what will happen now. We've got some difficult days ahead." His voice was low and sombre. His eyes blinked intently. The crowd was hushed for a moment.

"But it really doesn't matter with me now, because I've been to the mountaintop." Martin's voice began to rise. The audience began to cheer and shout "Yes, sir!" or "Yes, Doctor!"

"Like anybody, I would like to live a long life – longevity has its place," Martin continued. His eyes began to fill with tears. "But I'm not concerned about that now. I just want to do God's work. And He's allowed me to go up to the mountain. And I've looked over, and I've seen the promised land."

By now the crowd was whipped up into a frenzy. People whooped and cheered. Martin's passion became their passion.

"I may not get there with you. But I want you to know tonight, that we, as a people, will get to the promised land. And I'm happy tonight. I'm not worried about anything. I'm not fearing any man."

The audience was choked with emotion. There was a magical connection between them and this wonderful man up on the stage. He filled them with faith. Tonight, his words seemed especially brilliant.

Martin finished off with the words of a hymn. His voice sang out and filled the room.

"Mine eyes have seen the glory of the coming of the Lord." With that he turned promptly and left the stage.

The next evening Martin went out onto the balcony of his room at the Lorraine Motel to speak to his friend, the Reverend Jesse Jackson.

"Be sure to sing 'Precious Lord' tonight," Martin said. "And sing it well."

Martin bent down. A moment later there was a single rifle shot. Jesse looked on in disbelief. Martin was hit in the head. Jesse fell to his knees and scrambled on the balcony floor to help his friend. It looked bad... Martin had collapsed and there was blood everywhere. Jesse's whole body trembled as he felt for a pulse.

"If only... if only..." he muttered to himself, "if only he hadn't bent down... It'd have missed his face."

***

Back in Atlanta Martin's children, Yolanda, Martin, Dexter and Bernice, were watching television. Suddenly, there was a Special Bulletin from CBS News: "Dr. Martin Luther King Jr. has been shot in Memphis, at 6:01p.m" announced a serious voice.

The children looked at each other. They didn't say a word. Their minds began to race. What had happened? Was he alive? They ran up to their parents' bedroom. Their mother was on the phone to the Reverend Jesse Jackson.

"I understand," she said quietly, but calmly, into the telephone receiver. All she knew was that Martin had been shot. The children watched as their mother got ready to leave the house for the airport, to catch a plane to Memphis.

"Is Daddy coming back, Mommy?" asked Dexter.

"I don't know, darlings," answered Coretta,

stretching her arms around them in a group hug.

When Coretta reached the airport she heard the worst. Martin had been taken to a hospital in Memphis where he was pronounced dead. Numb with shock, Coretta turned back for home. Somehow, she had to tell her children they had lost their daddy.

Minutes after the news of Martin's death was reported, riots began in cities throughout America. Over the next few days there was violence and bloodshed as people expressed their pain. Meanwhile millions of other people mourned quietly the loss of a great man. On television they watched his final speech on the night before his death. Did he know he was going to die?

At his home in Atlanta his family struggled to come to terms with what had happened. Coretta was like a rock. She stayed calm and put on a brave face for the children. Once, she caught herself gazing at the artificial red carnations that Martin had sent her less than a month ago. The thought niggled her now as it had done then. Did he know? Did he know that he was going to die? Did he realize those flowers would have to last her a lifetime?

Meanwhile, the police in Memphis began the hunt for Martin's murderer. Witnesses told them about a well-dressed, white man who had dropped a rifle and escaped in a blue car. This man was James Earl Ray, and the police finally caught him at Heathrow Airport, London, England, in June 1968. The following year he pleaded guilty to assassinating Martin Luther King and was sentenced to 99 years in prison. Ray later claimed he was innocent. He said he was part of a government cover-up.

Ray died in prison in 1998 so we will probably never know if he was telling the truth.

***

Martin was buried in Atlanta on 9 April, 1968. More than 150,000 people followed his coffin which headed a procession through Atlanta to Ebenezer Baptist Church.

At the funeral all eyes were upon Martin's family. There was Coretta, his beautiful and dignified wife. She led her four children into the pew. Bernice, the youngest, sat on her lap. She was four and too young to understand what was going on. But, for the others, this was a dreadful day. Their daddy was gone.

Martin's voice filled the church. His final sermon had been taped and was played at the funeral service. For a moment, it was easy to believe that if you looked up he'd be in the pulpit. Most people kept their heads bowed. It was as if they were scared to look up and see that he really had gone. Once again, Martin's words had power and magic. They were wise and comforting. But there was something else in his words. Somehow it did seem that Martin knew he was about to die. He told people that they should remember him because he "gave his life for love".

***

In America, Martin Luther King's life and beliefs are remembered on the third Monday of January each year. "Martin Luther King Day" is a national holiday when people of all races and backgrounds come together. They remember Martin's dream of freedom for everyone. And, in the spirit of Martin Luther

King, they try to bring more love and understanding into the world.

TIMELINE

1929	*15 January*: Martin Luther King is born
1944	MLK admitted to Morehouse College aged 15
1948	MLK enters Crozer Theological Seminary. *25 February*: ordained to the Baptist ministry
1945	Marries Coretta Scott and settles in Montgomery, Alabama
1955	Joins the bus boycott after Rosa Parks is arrested and becomes official spokesman for the boycott.
1956	*November 13*: Supreme Court rules that bus segregation is illegal
1958	On a speaking tour MLK is stabbed in Harlem but survives
1959	MLK resigns from the Dexter Avenue Baptist church, where he is pastor, to concentrate on Civil Rights full-time
1960	Lunch counter sit-ins in North Carolina. MLK is arrested, sentenced to 4 months in prison but released

	through the intervention of John and Robert Kennedy'
1961	Segregation on interstate travel banned due to MLK and the Freedom Riders' campaign
1963	The March on Washington – the largest Civil Rights demonstration in history attended by nearly 250,000. MLK makes his famous *"I have a dream"* speech *November 22:* President Kennedy assassinated
1964	MLK is *Time* magazine's Man of the Year; awarded Nobel Peace Prize
1968	*April 4*: Memphis, MLK is assassinated

QUIZ

After you've finished the book, test yourself and see how well you remember what you've read.

1. The period when Martin Luther King was born is known as:
   The Great Depression
   The Black Hole
   The Dark Ages

2. For what accomplishment did Martin win a prize at the age of 14?
   Public speaking
   Javelin throwing
   Life drawing

3. How did Martin spend his holidays during the summer of 1944?
   Working on a tobacco farm in Connecticut
   Learning how to scuba dive in Florida
   Travelling with his family in Europe

4. When Martin crossed the border to the Southern US on his return journey from Connecticut:
   The waiter made him sit behind a curtain at the

back of the train's dining car
His luggage was searched for contraband
He met an old friend who welcomed him with open arms

5. What did Martin's father want him to become when he grew up?
   A preacher
   A painter
   A palaeontologist

6. What subject did Crozer College specialise in?
   Theology
   Zoology
   Astrology

7. Martin and his friend Philip spent their weekends when they were at Boston University:
   Going to jazz clubs and talking about philosophy
   Fly-fishing and making needlework cushions
   Cooking meals for their friends and learning ancient Greek

8. What was Coretta Scott studying when she met Martin?
   Gymnastics
   Singing
   Mathematics

9. The nickname Martin gave his daughter Yolanda was:
   Yoyo
   Yoki
   Yoko

10. How many years did the NAACP have to battle before segregation was banned in state-funded schools?
   4
   14
   44

11. What did the black population of Montgomery decide to do when Rosa Parks was arrested?
   Boycott the bus service
   Break into the police station
   Refuse to go to work

12. On 17 May, 1957, 25,000 black Americans gathered in front of the Lincoln Memorial in Washington DC to ask for:
   The right to vote
   The right to own guns
   The right to drive a car

13. In order for black children to attend Little Rock High School in safety, the federal government:
   Installed fire alarms in every classroom

Sent 1,000 paratroopers to escort them
Paid for them to attend self-defence classes

14. What did the black students who sat down at segregated lunch counters hope would happen?
   That they would be arrested and taken to jail
   That they would be served quickly so they could get back to their studies
   That McDonald's would lower their prices because they were losing business

15. What sentence did Martin receive for a minor traffic offence?
   Four months' hard labour
   Three points on his driving licence
   $100 fine

16. Who said, "Ask not what your country can do for you – ask what you can do for your country"?
   Martin Luther King
   John Fitzgerald Kennedy
   Dolly Parton

17. Where was the Civil Rights campaign of 1963 launched?
   Birmingham, Alabama
   London, Ohio
   Manchester, New Hampshire

18. What did the police do when thousands of children went on a protest march?
   Set dogs on them and put them in jail
   Rang their parents and took them home
   Told their teachers to give them detention every night for a week

19. Which of these film stars went on the great March on Washington for Jobs and Freedom in 1963?
   Marlon Brando
   George Clooney
   Johnny Depp

20. Before he went away for work, Martin always gave Coretta:
   Flowers
   Chocolates
   Perfume

Author Biography

A former music journalist, Liz Gogerly now writes children's books. Among her most popular titles are biographies on Elvis Presley (Hodder Wayland), Hitler and Sigmund Freud (Watts). She is also the author of *Who Was... John Lennon* (Short Books, 2005) She lives in Brighton and has a young son.

Other titles in the WHO WAS... series:

MOZART
Child Genius
Gill Hornby

By the time he was four years old, it was clear that Wolfgang Amadeus Mozart was a musical genius. He could already play the clavier, the organ and the violin to perfection. When he was just seven, little Mozart began touring Europe, performing at court to Kings and Queens, and in concert halls to crowds of the paying public.

His father could see that his little Wolfgang would one day change the face of European music, and presumed that the adult Mozart would be wealthy, famous, adored around the world. What he did not know was how hard it can be for a child genius to grow up...

ISBN: 1-904977-64-2

BOUDICCA
Warrior Queen
Siân Busby

As Queen of Icenia in 1st Century AD Britain, married to her beloved Prasutagus, Boudicca lived a wonderful life. But then, after her husband weakened and died, and, with the ever-expanding Roman Empire making ever more impossible demands on her, young Boudicca was forced to stand up and defend her people.

Fearless and unprepared to compromise, Boudicca saw nothing to stop her going to war on her own. For her, slavery to Rome was not an option, even if this meant bloodshed and almost inevitable death...

ISBN: 1-904977-59-6